Reimagining the Recipe for Research & Innovation

The Secret Sauce of Social Science

ACADEMY of SOCIAL SCIENCES | CAMPAIGN for SOCIAL SCIENCE

The Academy of Social Sciences promotes social sciences in the UK for public benefit. We showcase, champion and advocate for the social sciences, raising awareness of their immense influence and evidence-based insights, helping to secure a flourishing future for them.

The Academy's Campaign for Social Science demonstrates how social science improves public policy, society and all our lives. It highlights the value of applied social science research and advocates for its greater use in decision-making and in government.

To contact us, please email:
media@acss.org.uk for media enquiries
office@acss.org.uk for general enquiries
Or call +44 (0) 300 303 3513

For further information, see:
www.acss.org.uk
X (formerly Twitter): @AcadSocSciences and @CfSocialScience

The Academy of Social Sciences is a company registered in England, number 3847936, and a registered charity, number 1088537

ACADEMY
of SOCIAL
SCIENCES

CAMPAIGN
for SOCIAL
SCIENCE

Reimagining the Recipe for Research & Innovation

The Secret Sauce of Social Science

James Wilsdon

Kathryn Weber-Boer

Juergen Wastl

Ed Bridges

§ Sage

Academy of Social Sciences
c/o Knox Cropper LLP
5 Floor, 65 Leadenhall Street
London, EC3A 2AD
+44 (0) 300 303 3513

1 Oliver's Yard
55 City Road
London EC1Y 1SP

2455 Teller Road
Thousand Oaks
California 91320

Unit No 323-333, Third Floor, F-Block
International Trade Tower, Nehru Place
New Delhi 110 019

8 Marina View Suite 43-053
Asia Square Tower 1
Singapore 018960

Printed in the UK

British Library Cataloguing in Publication data

A catalogue record for this book is available from the British Library

ISBN 978-1-5296-8195-6 (web PDF)
DOI: 10.4135/wp.240118

About the authors

James Wilsdon FAcSS is Professor of Research Policy at University College London (UCL) and Executive Director of the Research on Research Institute (RoRI). ORCID: 0000-0002-5395-5949

Kathryn Weber-Boer is D&A Hub - Technical Product Specialist at Digital Science. ORCID: 0000-0002-4495-3001

Juergen Wastl is VP Research Evaluation & Global Challenges at Digital Science. ORCID: 0000-0001-7757-8001

Ed Bridges is Head of Policy & Public Affairs at the Academy of Social Sciences.

To cite this report: Wilsdon, J., Weber-Boer, K., Wastl, J. and Bridges, E. (2023). *Reimagining the recipe for research and innovation: the secret sauce of social science*. London. Sage/Academy of Social Sciences.

Contents

Introduction

'secret sauce (n): an element, quality, ability, or practice that makes something or someone successful or distinctive.'

(Merriam-Webster online dictionary definition of 'secret sauce')

It is widely acknowledged that the UK has a high-performing research base. For a country of 69 million people, the UK benefits from a larger-than-average share of leading universities. These support a broader innovation system, with strengths in a number of science areas, including biomedical and pharmaceutical research and development (R&D), defence and aerospace, digital technologies and artificial intelligence (AI). Public R&D investment has risen in three years by around 25%.

While the UK scientific talent pool runs deep, so do its strengths in social sciences, which also boast a breadth of expertise which is vital to the needs of the UK economy and society. Areas of strength from social science disciplines include (but are not limited to) leadership, strategic planning, international liaison, sustainability, consumer growth, productivity and labour markets, human behaviour, marketing, legal and financial management, policy analysis, education, city and regional planning, and climate change adaptation.

But there are weaknesses too. In relative terms, the UK under-invests in research and innovation (R&I), particularly from the private sector, whilst public investment remains vulnerable to wider economic pressures. Meanwhile, the UK's public R&I system is weighted to London and the southeast of England, and is heavily reliant on universities, with limited regional and institutional diversity. Overall productivity – including R&D productivity – has lagged since the 2008 financial crisis. These weaknesses are exacerbated by the impacts of Brexit, COVID-19 and the war in Ukraine.

R&I currently enjoys high levels of support across the political spectrum. Since becoming Prime Minister, Rishi Sunak has championed a vision for the UK as a 'science and technology superpower', following the lead set by his predecessor, Boris Johnson. Heightened political engagement has been accompanied by a wholesale reorganisation of R&I governance and institutions over the past five years (including a new Whitehall Department for Science Innovation and Technology).

Alongside, there have been a series of significant policy and strategic reviews, including Sir Paul Nurse's landscape review, an independent review of UK

Research and Innovation (UKRI), a new Science & Technology Framework, an International Technology Strategy, a review of pro-innovation regulation, a refreshed Integrated Review of security, defence, development and foreign policy (with prominent emphasis on science and technology); and ambitious plans for international R&I collaboration, which we now know will also include association to Horizon Europe. At a devolved level, we have seen a new Innovation Strategy for Wales, and a National Strategy for Economic Transformation in Scotland with a strong focus on R&I.

So the UK system has been in a period of flux, as new institutions, priorities and investments find their niche in a landscape which was already crowded and complex. The need for more interdisciplinarity, integration and creative synthesis across R&D is one of a number of cross-cutting objectives being pursued – particularly through the Grant Review of UKRI. The ground for this had already been laid by the 2021 Spending Review settlement, which gave UKRI greater flexibility in its approach to funding multi- and interdisciplinary research, with cross-cutting funds increasingly being allocated through a shared pool. This is welcome and is something that may receive further emphasis in future spending reviews.

Nevertheless, a striking feature of recent initiatives and announcements is the visible priority they place on new technologies and STEM-related R&I, and the limited amount that they say about the role and contribution of the social sciences. In some technology fields, there are sound reasons for this targeted focus, but UK R&I policy and strategy is now at risk of becoming lopsided and missing an equivalently rich, textured and ambitious agenda for the many ways social science research and expertise contribute to addressing the UK's economic, social and environmental priorities.

Within this context, we suggest that there is a critical yet under-explored role for the social sciences within the UK's research, development and innovation system, as a 'secret sauce' which can elevate research into a recipe that is genuinely unique and world-leading.

The dictionary definition of 'secret sauce' is 'an element, quality, ability, or practice that makes something or someone successful or distinctive'. The social sciences are not something to be added to (or 'poured over') STEM research before serving it up to society. Rather, they are catalysing ingredients, bringing out the full flavour of STEM research and adding their own notes as well. In line with our 'secret sauce' analogy, this report sets out four ingredients which the social sciences bring, drawing on data that highlights the ways in which social scientists contribute to a diverse menu of talent and impact. The four ingredients can be summarised as follows:

1. **Social sciences enable whole-systems thinking.** They enable innovators and entrepreneurs to understand system capabilities, vital system contexts and dynamics – including economies, productivity, institutions, skills, training and cultures – as well as playing a role in understanding and improving the R&I system itself.

2. **Social sciences are critical for good policy development.** Social science plays a disproportionately significant role in informing policy, and consistently delivers for governments when developing evidence-based policy.

3. **Social sciences underpin smart and responsible innovation.** Emerging technologies depend upon social sciences for the legal, regulatory and ethical frameworks that are essential for their efficacy and adoption within a UK context.

4. **Social sciences are essential to international collaboration and tackling shared global challenges.** The UK's international R&I strategy is outwardly focused and benefits from being underpinned by social sciences (e.g., business and management, politics, geography, international development). The UK's social scientists have a track record of working effectively with partners and providing a substantive focus for UK strengths and strategic advantage (e.g., in relation to sustainable development goals (SDGs), global challenges, etc.).

Methodological approach

The approach we adopted was to examine how social science and STEM research interact when cross-disciplinary research outcomes are identified. To understand the breadth and depth of collaborative research in the UK, we employed 'out-of-the-box' elements of Digital Science's Dimensions' database, specifically:

- Landmark research analysis, particularly focusing on citations of cross-disciplinary research involving social science and STEM;
- Cluster analysis, based on existing published work in relevant areas;
- Research trajectory analysis for STEM, social sciences and cross-disciplinary research from both.

These approaches are explained and unpacked further in relation to each of these examples given; the Boolean searches used to query the Dimensions datasets can be found in Appendix A.

By definition, this emphasis on understanding social sciences' interaction with STEM means that the four themes explored in the report have a heavy focus on technology, and often on those areas of emerging technology which feature strongly in governments' thinking about research and innovation. In making this our focus for the current report, we are conscious that it leaves a swathe of valuable social science disciplines under-represented in our analysis. Nevertheless, it tells an important story about the broad role of social sciences within the research and innovation ecosystem.

INGREDIENT 1:
Social sciences enable whole-systems thinking

By their nature, social scientists are intellectually engaged with the relationships and connections between different systems and seek through their work to understand and explain them. This 'systems thinking' approach is strongly visible in the social sciences, with social scientists bringing an understanding of the human capabilities and dynamics of systems – including of economies, productivity, institutions, skills, training, behaviours and cultures.

However, there is a danger of the social sciences being seen as an add-on or afterthought to STEM research – or, indeed, as an 'ELSIfication', whereby social scientists' contributions are limited to identifying or ameliorating the potentially negative ethical, legal or societal implications (ELSI) of scientific or technological advances.[1] Our argument in this report is that social scientists have an essential role to play across the entire recipe, catalysing the development of new flavours, rather than simply being a garnish to a dish created by STEM.

It is clear that the impact of the social sciences on scientific practice arises both from engagement in the subject of research (e.g., the role of psychologists in improving the perception, and therefore performance, of robotic health assistants), and from an interrogation of the assumptions and consequences of that research. Some notable examples of this effect are the contribution of legal studies to the development of legal frameworks for data protection, efforts to reduce or ameliorate digital inequalities, and the use of psychological research to improve virtual learning environments. Social sciences play a role not only in improving new technologies, but in understanding and anticipating the broader societal effect of those technologies and the scientific practices that produce them.

To explore the influence of specific social sciences, one can zoom into some of the technologies that have grown out of AI. One such example is that of trustworthy autonomous systems (TAS), which is a useful microcosm of the broader impact and influence of the social sciences. Table 1 shows three emerging areas of study within TAS, over the period 2012–2022, looking at the contribution of UK-affiliated research relative to the global research contribution.

---

[1] See, for example, articles by Williams (2006) on pitfalls in assessing high technology futures, or Stilgoe, Lock & Wilsdon (2014) on the need to promote public engagement with science. For full references, refer to the selected academic bibliography in Appendix C at the end of the report.

The UK provides a greater-than-average contribution to many of these areas. The UK's average yearly share of global publications is 4%; the share for these topics is near or more than double that value here.

Table 1: The UK's contribution to global research in three emerging areas of study within trustworthy autonomous systems

	Digital health technologies*	Autonomous systems, AI and ethics	Responsible AI
Social Sciences Fields	11.9% (1,922 / 16,114)	7.9% (2,316 / 29,499)	7.7% (186 / 2,402)
Mixed Fields	14.0% (3,681 / 26,254)	14.0% (370 / 2,640)	10.3% (43 / 418)
STEM Fields	14.5% (11,255 / 77,408)	12.2% (8,707 / 71,384)	7.9% (1,341 / 17,055)

*"Digital health technologies" in this document refers to publications in the field of Information and Computing Sciences where the title or abstract contain the phrases "mental health", "digital health technology" or "digital mental health".

The social sciences (not just in the fields of human society, but also economics, law, education and others) are integral parts of the wider research ecosystem, including in fields where a lay audience might not expect them to feature prominently. The UK is delivering strong research on digital health technologies, due in no small part to contributions from our social science research base. The same is true for research on autonomous systems, AI and ethics. UK-affiliated research in many of the social sciences contributes disproportionately to these areas of study.

Tables 2 and 3 show the fields in which the UK's share of publications was over 8% of the global number of publications in the given field (and where there were more than 65 papers published on the subject in the UK), or where the average citation per publication was over twice the global average number of citations per paper. A full table of publication counts by field, and the keywords used to identify the publications, can be found in Appendix B. Across Tables 2 and 3, we see contributions from the field of health psychology – in Table 2 to digital health technology (14.2% of global average publications), and in Table 3 to autonomous systems, AI and ethics (15.7% of global average publications). In both cases, these are close to contributions from STEM disciplines, and

Case study: AIDS and youth in the developing world

Social sciences intrinsically understand the interconnected nature of society, and the ways in which solving a given social problem depends on also addressing a complex web of other challenges. This is nowhere better showcased than through the work of Prof. Lucie Cluver, whose work on children and young people affected by AIDS in South Africa has led to major systemic social change at the interface of health, poverty, education, behaviour and policy.

By 2008, 12 million children in sub-Saharan Africa were orphaned by AIDS. Cross-sectional studies showed psychological problems for AIDS-orphaned children, but no longitudinal study had explored the enduring psychological effects of AIDS-orphanhood in the developing world. The Orphan Resilience Study followed over 1,000 children over four years to identify impacts of orphanhood. The results indicated that AIDS-orphaned children showed higher depression, anxiety and post-traumatic stress disorder scores when compared with their peers. The study concluded that negative mental health outcomes amongst AIDS-orphaned children were maintained and worsened over a four-year period, and recommended that psychosocial support programmes be sustained, and focus on youth as well as young children.

This work then informed the Young Carers Study, the world's largest study of risk and resilience amongst AIDS-affected children. Across three South African provinces, the study interviewed 6,000 children and 1,500 of their parents or guardians about their access to social welfare grants, health visitors, and free school meals. The research suggested that children who live with AIDS-sufferers suffered as much psychological distress as those who have been orphaned by AIDS, and that this had a direct impact on school attendance.

The work led to a long-standing set of partnerships with the South African government, including further research into whether social support grants could reduce HIV risks amongst young girls. Many teenage girls were living in desperate poverty and felt that they had little choice but to find an older boyfriend to help them pay for food and basic items for their families. Research showed that introducing a government social benefit of around $20 per month reduced the need for girls to enter relationships with 'Sugar Daddies' as a way of helping their families deal with desperate poverty. Such cash benefits could reduce girls' risk of infection by up to 50%.

reflect social sciences' important contribution. In digital health technologies, the fields of applied and developmental psychology and clinical and health psychology have played an important role. These areas of psychology straddle the categories of STEM and the social sciences, but the relationship between concepts (shown in Figure 1) demonstrates the interdisciplinarity of this research: ranging from natural language processing to social touch.

Table 2: The UK's contribution to global research in digital health technologies (see Appendix B)

Digital health technologies*			
		UK publications relative to global total	UK average citation relative to global average
Social Sciences Fields		**11.9%**	
	Economics	13.9% (84 / 605)	105.8% (22.8 / 21.6)
	Education	12.6% (254 / 2,018)	108.0% (12.4 / 11.4)
	Human Society	13.5% (1,193 / 8,869)	113.7% (16.7 / 14.7)
Mixed Fields		**14.0%**	
	Psychology	14.2% (3,633 / 25,619)	135.6% (30 / 22.1)
STEM Fields		**14.5%**	
	Biomedical & Clinical Sciences	15.3% (3,128 / 20,484)	142.7% (32.1 / 22.5)
	Health Sciences	15.4% (7,522 / 48,853)	127.3% (22.3 / 17.5)

* "Digital health technologies" in this document refers to publications in the field of Information and Computing Sciences where the title or abstract contain the phrases "mental health", "digital health technology" or "digital mental health".

Figure 1: Concept network graph for UK research into digital mental health in the fields of Psychology and Information and Computing Sciences (2012-2022)

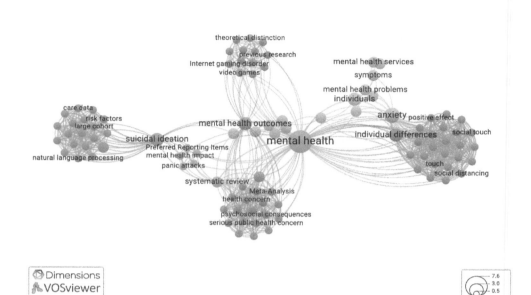

Source: Dimensions from Digital Science

The average citations of UK-affiliated papers relative to the global average citation of papers in these areas for the years 2012–2022 (the average number of citations is thus 100%) shows that the UK has a disproportionately high scholarly impact in these areas of study within the fields of the social sciences. Again, the contribution of the field of human society is not only proportionally larger (as shown in Table 2), but also more highly cited than average. The field of legal studies has been highly influential in autonomous systems, AI and ethics, although with a relative contribution of only 6.3% (as shown in Table 3).

Table 3: The UK's contribution to global research in autonomous systems, AI and ethics

Autonomous systems, AI and ethics		UK share of publications	Percentage of global average citation
Social Sciences Fields			
	Built Environment & Design	**9.7%** (86 / 887)	187.0% (24.0 / 12.9)
	Economics	**10.2%** (102 / 1,003)	195.5% (11.7 / 6.0)
	Education	7.0% (162 / 2,322)	**216.6%** (11.2 / 5.2)
	Human Society	**11.7%** (605 / 10,786)	**225.1%** (17.4 / 7.7)
	Law & Legal Studies	6.3% (680 / 10,786)	**263.5%** (9.0 / 3.4)
Mixed Fields			
	Psychology	**15.7%** (328 / 2,093)	173.0% (17.4 / 10.0)
STEM Fields			
	Agricultural, Veterinary & Food Sciences	**14.1%** (78 / 552)	96.8% (10.0 / 10.3)
	Biological Sciences	**11.5%** (209 / 1,823)	160.7% (10.0 / 10.3)
	Biomedical & Clinical Sciences	**14.2%** (3,158 / 22,187)	157.8% (12.3 / 7.8)
	Health Sciences	**19.9%** (3,174 / 15,961)	144.0% (12.0 / 8.3)
	Mathematical Sciences	**8.4%** (74 / 886)	165.0% (12.0 / 7.3)

What is most notable about the average citation rate of UK-based research on autonomous systems, AI and ethics is that three of the fields of the social sciences (education, human society and law and legal studies) are cited over twice the global average for papers with the same combination of field and subject. This is a threshold which the STEM fields listed in Table 3 have not reached. This means that, although the UK-based STEM fields are very active in the area of autonomous systems, AI and ethics, their influence on the topic in their field is approximately average, whereas many of the UK-based social sciences have a greater influence on these areas of study. In the years 2012–2022, UK publications had an average of 20.7 citations per publication, while that number globally was 8.7 citations per publication.

Thus, the UK has, on average, a citation rate at least 238% higher than the global norm. Looking at publications which can be attributed to the social science or STEM fields, or identified as cross-disciplinary publications (STEMSocSci in Table 4), **the average citations per paper is 240% higher in the UK social sciences than globally, 190% higher in STEM fields, and 188% higher in cross-disciplinary publications.**

Table 4: Average citations per paper (citation rate) for research publications

Region	SocSci	STEM	STEMSocSci
Global	6.5	12.4	10.6
UK	15.6	23.5	19.9

Policy and administration (a field within human society) similarly produced a high number of publications (128) and average citations per paper (18.5) in the area of autonomous systems, AI and ethics. The concept co-occurrence network (see Figure 10 in Appendix B) shows the concepts that are most common in UK-based research about autonomous systems, AI and ethics in the field of policy and administration (2012–2022). It shows that social science research is grappling with the social implications of this technology, and working to understand its consequences, capabilities and appropriate restrictions. We also looked into adjacent topics e.g. responsible AI (see Table 11 in Appendix B for further details).

Taking another example of emerging technologies, research on the virtual classroom (online learning and education technologies), a highly pertinent topic to the social science field of education, is also a focus of study across multiple STEM and social science fields. As Table 5 shows, the field of human society is again highly represented in the UK, as is psychology. It is interesting to note that both STEM and social science-related fields have a disproportionately high scholarly impact in rates of citation, with several fields surpassing 200% of the global average citations. The fields of law and legal studies, environmental studies, chemical science, earth science and the physical sciences each have more than three times the rate of citation of global publications in their field on this subject. That said, it is striking that the UK contributes only an average share of publications in most of these areas, with only biomedical and clinical and health sciences reaching the 8% mark. It indicates that the impact relative to contribution is particularly high for UK-based research on the subject of online learning.

Table 5: UK and Global Share of Publications on Online Learning

Online learning		UK share of publications	Percentage of global average citation
Social Sciences Fields			
	Built Environment & Design	4.4% (257 / 5,860)	**255.3%** (15.8 / 6.2)
	Commerce, Management, Tourism & Services	3.7% (614 / 16,525)	**286.3%** (17.4 / 6.1)
	Education	3.2% (4,094 / 127,455)	**246.9%** (14.0 / 5.7)
	Human Society	4.3% (727 / 16,896)	**247.6%** (14.2 / 5.7)
	Law & Legal Studies	3.2% (128 / 4,015)	**353.5%** (8.0 / 2.3)
Mixed Fields			
	Environmental Sciences	5.6% (115 / 2,060)	**337.1%** (28.6 / 8.5)

(Table 5 continued)

	Psychology	5.3% (384 / 7,502)	184.8% (25.4 / 13.8)
STEM Fields			
	Agriculture, Veterinary & Food Sciences	3.5% (97 / 2,755)	**212.0%** (15.4 / 7.3)
	Biomedical & Clinical Sciences	**9.4%** (2,234 / 23,725)	174.1% (19.6 / 11.2)
	Earth Sciences	2.3% (84 / 3,621)	**394.8%** (16.9 / 4.3)
	Engineering	2.8% (561 / 19,823)	**255.9%** (17.5 / 6.8)
	Health Sciences	**8.9%** (2,297 / 25,900)	193.4% (20.13 / 10.41)
	Information & Computing Sciences	3.2% (2,253 / 70,886)	**238.8%** (14.52 / 6.08)

Figure 2 is a concept co-occurrence network for UK-based research into online learning and education technologies. It covers research which is categorised as simultaneously belonging to the fields of health sciences and education. Again, the network shows the number of UK-based publications relating to online learning which have dealt significantly with the given concept (the size of the points) and when that concept occurred in combination with another (the lines linking concepts).

The concept of 'skills' has been highlighted here. The network, as a whole, highlights the range of this research, including technologies (resources, information technology, communication technologies), social conditions (emotional challenges, mental health and subjectivity) and practical concerns (professional development, skills, educational tools). The concepts united by an association with 'skills' indicate that this research is actively engaged with issues that range from pedagogy to future planning to mental health.

Figure 2: Concept network graph for UK research into online learning

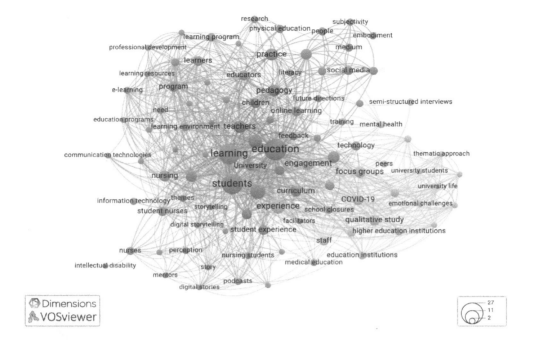

Source: Dimensions from Digital Science

Learning points

- The social sciences don't just improve technologies; they also shape how we understand and engage with them, because of social sciences' strength in understanding and interpreting systems.
- The social sciences play an important and integral role in responsible scientific innovation.
- UK social sciences research is influential in the study of significant emerging technologies. It is further evidence that the UK is a world leader in social science research because of the breadth and depth of our social science base.

INGREDIENT 2:
Social sciences are critical for good policy development

Social science research lies at the heart of good public policy. It can define and diagnose the most acute challenges facing society and identify the policy levers to address them. The UK Government recognises this in its list of Areas of Research Interest, with social science research lying at the heart of many priorities. Drawing on a wealth of evidence from across disciplines, social scientists will be key to boosting economic productivity, developing training that fulfils society's needs, and promoting adaptation and further cycles of innovation and growth.

Our data show that the research of social scientists plays a disproportionately high role in informing policy. When we look at translation through from grants to publications to citations in policy documents, we see social science research consistently delivering for governments when developing evidence-based policy. We looked at the research cited by policy documents from UK governmental organisations and analysed their source to see whether they arose from STEM, social science or other publications, as well as looking at the category of the supporting grants. Overall, approximately 3% of publications produced with the support of grants involving STEM fields end up cited by policy documents, whereas that number rises to 6% of publications supported by grants involving the social sciences and 7.5% of publications supported by grants that can be categorised as jointly involving STEM and the social science fields.

Looking at Table 6, we can also see that, in comparing the total number of grants and publications resulting in research relevant to government policymaking, the effect of social sciences on policy is accomplished with a proportionally smaller number of grants and papers relative to the non-health-related STEM fields.

Table 6: Policy documents citing UK-based publications, count of cited publications, and count of grants supporting those publications

	Grants	Publications	Policy documents
Social Sciences	1,781	1,459	1,617
STEM	2,458	2,263	999
SocSci/STEM	475	451	144

Our analysis uses a classification of grants, publications and policy documents, by their respective discipline, to enable an examination of the flow throughout the research life cycle, from grant award to citation by policymakers. The three alluvial diagrams shown in Figure 3 indicate the relative contribution of the social sciences and STEM fields to policy documents produced by policy institutions across the UK.[2] From left to right, they show: the number of grants per category, the number of publications per category and the number of policy documents per category.

Figure 3: Contribution by category to specific UK government policymakers, by grants (A), publications (B), and policy documents (C)

A

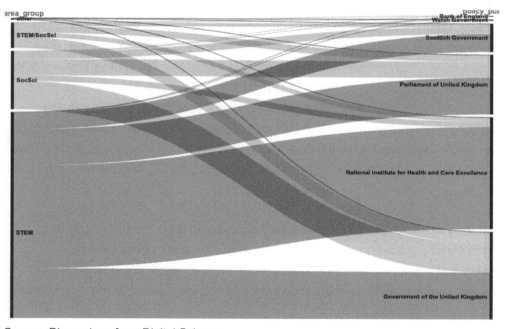

Source: Dimensions from Digital Science

[2] The diagrams in Figure 3 show policy documents published between 2012 and 2022 and only includes those publications where grants, publications and policy documents could each be related to STEM or social science fields. UK governmental institutions included in the Dimension dataset are: UK Government, UK Parliament, Senedd Cymru, Scottish Government, the Bank of England and the National Institute for Health and Care Excellence.

B

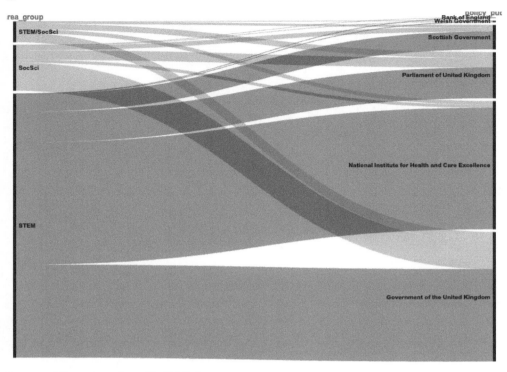

Source: Dimensions from Digital Science

C

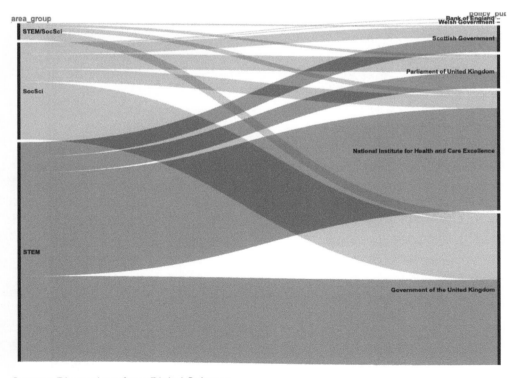

Source: Dimensions from Digital Science

Case study: Informing and explaining the science of climate change

Good policy development depends on securing public support and public consent, often for things that are complex to understand or require changes in how people live their lives. For those tasked with tackling climate change, social science has a critical role to play in explaining the need for (and the mechanics of) climate adaptation to sceptical or indifferent sections of the public.

The Centre for Climate Change & Social Transformations (CAST) is a global hub for understanding the systemic and society-wide transformations that are required to address climate change. Based in the UK and based on a partnership of five universities and one charity, CAST researches and develops the social transformations needed to produce a low-carbon and sustainable society, asking how society can live differently – and better – in ways that meet the urgent need for rapid and far-reaching emission reductions. Recent work by CAST has examined different generational attitudes to climate change, psychological factors affecting people's views on low emission zones and the barriers to encouraging people to eat less meat in their diets.

CAST's Director, Prof. Lorraine Whitmarsh, has argued that progress towards reducing emissions so far has depended on shifting energy supply towards lower carbon energy resources – but that further progress depends on reducing rapidly demand for energy by changing how we live. Despite this, the scale of behaviour change is not yet recognised by the public – with most people wrongly thinking that recycling, reducing food waste and saving some energy will be enough. Only by persuading the public to change their behaviours and helping them to feel ownership of the issue can change happen, with perceptions of fairness being critical to public acceptance of climate change.

By the same token, the Place-based Climate Action Network (PCAN) seeks to translate climate policy into action 'on the ground' in communities by bringing together the research community and decision-makers in the public, private and third sectors. A PCAN report in 2019 not only provided a comprehensive review of UK-funded social science research on climate change over the last ten years, but also identified some important research gaps, including the need for better understanding of:

- Poverty alleviation in a zero-carbon world, to inform the ongoing debate about (real and perceived) trade-offs between emissions reductions and poverty alleviation.
- The role of sustainable finance, reflecting the fact that redirecting financial flows towards zero-carbon, climate-resilient investment is one of the biggest levers in the fight against climate change.

What we can see from the diagrams is that although most of the grants and publications used by governmental policymakers arise from STEM fields, the translation rate from grants into publications and then into policy documents is much higher for the social sciences than it is for STEM. The diagrams indicate that the bulk of STEM-related grants and publications arise from the health sciences and biomedical and clinical sciences, as can be seen in comparison with Figure 4.

The impact of social science research on governmental policymaking in the UK is further demonstrated by examining the high degree of exchange across disciplinary fields. The alluvial diagram in Figure 4 shows the number of policy documents per grant category (on the left) and per publication category (in the middle), with the fields of health sciences and biomedical and clinical sciences removed.[3] What we see is that policy documents in every category draw upon grants and publications produced in the others. Notably, nearly half of UK policy documents in the years 2012–2022 drew on SocSci-related or joint SocSci/STEM grants.

---

[3] This was done because of the enlarged effect of the Health and Clinical Sciences on policy over the period under investigation.

Figure 4: Contribution to specific UK government policymakers by category of policy document of grants and publications, excluding the health sciences

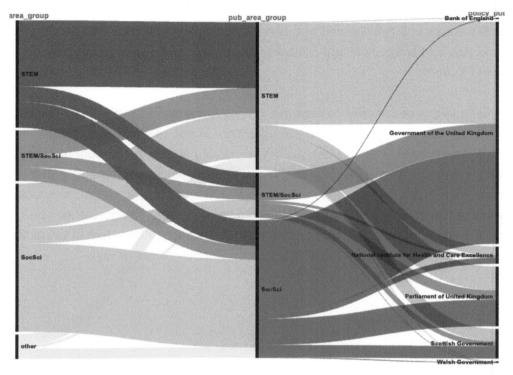

Source: Dimensions from Digital Science

The diagrams show a mutually beneficial cross-pollination of grants and publications. STEM and social science both have a wide reach in terms of the policymaking organisations citing their work, as well as there being strong flows between STEM and social science on the journey from grants to publication and into policy.

Learning points
- The translation rate from grants into publications and then into policy documents is much higher for the social sciences than it is for STEM.
- It is clear that research which influences public policy draws heavily from both the social sciences and STEM, and that there are strong flows between disciplines along their journey.
- The policy focus and societal relevance of the social science lens makes them uniquely well placed to help apply academic research for the public good.

INGREDIENT 3:
Social sciences underpin smart and responsible innovation

'To ensure we become an AI superpower, though, it is crucial that we do all we can to create the right environment to harness the benefits of AI and remain at the forefront of technological developments. That includes getting regulation right so that innovators can thrive and the risks posed by AI can be addressed. These risks could include anything from physical harm, an undermining of national security, as well as risks to mental health. The development and deployment of AI can also present ethical challenges which do not always have clear answers. … Unless we build public trust, we will miss out on many of the benefits on offer.'

(Michelle Donelan MP, UK Government Secretary of State for Science, Innovation & Technology, June 2023 in her foreword to <u>A pro-innovation approach to AI regulation</u>)

As illustrated by high-profile debates in the past year about the societal implications of AI-based applications like ChatGPT, technological progress depends on effective and anticipatory governance of the opportunities and uncertainties of innovation.

After a period in which such perspectives were downplayed, UK policymakers are once again emphasising governance as a crucial enabler for innovation rather than an obstacle. These challenges cannot be adequately addressed without the participation of the social sciences. Through their understanding of human behaviour, public opinion, legal systems, markets and public policy, social scientists can help to ensure the responsible and sustainable development of new technologies, and anticipate and reduce problems of social acceptance or heightened inequalities.

Science and technology are unpredictable, yet have a tendency to 'lock-in' to particular trajectories before there is clear evidence on which to understand their ramifications. These trajectories often become clear only when it is too late to change direction. When a technology like ChatGPT or genome editing begins to be publicly significant, it is not clear who is in charge, or what the rules should be that govern its development and use. Policymakers often prefer to wait until more is known about the benefits and risks, or to rely on science's own well-evolved systems of self-governance. But past lessons and surprises suggest that these approaches are insufficient to secure public trust or guarantee outcomes in the public interest.

A first step towards improving governance is to recognise that alternatives are available. Here the social sciences are crucial. For example, different countries can take very different approaches to governing biotechnology. Sheila Jasanoff has described how the US system for biotechnology focuses on the products of innovation, while the European approach targets the process of innovation. In some sectors and countries, the precautionary principle provides a legal basis for governance. By contrast, digital and internet companies tend to be governed in a reactive way, inheriting a model from Silicon Valley that presumes benefits are clear. As the scale and power of companies such as Meta, Google and Amazon continue to grow, governments have realised the limitations of this model, giving rise to what Geoff Mulgan has described as 'a new field of 'anticipatory regulation'.'

The social sciences also help us to make sense of public reactions to technological change, which may range from enthusiasm to hostility, uncertainty to ambivalence. People typically want to know who is likely to benefit, what the risks might be, who is making the decisions and what will happen if things go wrong. And public attitudes and governance are inextricably linked. People are not only concerned with questions of risk and safety. They are also interested in who is likely to win and lose.

Social science research over the last three decades has led to important changes in how governments and businesses approach public engagement with science and technology. Whereas scientific institutions used to prioritise communication, explanation and public awareness, they now tend to stress the need for dialogue.

A further example of the distinct flavour of the social sciences being integral can be found within law, which has had a significant scholarly impact on the topics of autonomous systems, AI and ethics (with an average citation rate of more than 2.5 times the global average in its field). Indeed, a single publication (Wachter, Mittelstadt & Russell, 2021: Why fairness cannot be automated: bridging the gap between EU non-discrimination law and AI) in the subfield of international and comparative law has a geometric mean FCR of 213.86.[4] In its own words, this paper 'addresses this critical gap between legal, technical, and organisational notions of algorithmic fairness'.

---

[4] The Field Citation Ratio (FCR) is a citation-based measure of scientific influence of one or more articles. It is calculated by dividing the number of citations a paper has received by the average number received by documents published in the same year and in the same Fields of Research (FoR) category. For more information, read 'What is the FCR? How is it calculated?

Case study: Artificial Intelligence and robotics

Although artificial intelligence, data science, machine learning and robotics are all closely associated with STEM subjects and skills, the expertise of social scientists is fundamental to ensuring new technologies can fit with the world around us and have the greatest impact on our daily lives.

Our report makes reference to an influential paper from 2021 which we argue acts as a portmanteau of the type of social scientific thinking which is essential for STEM outputs to be adapted and adopted. The article identified an incompatibility between European notions of discrimination and existing work on algorithmic and automated fairness, making three key arguments:

- The law (EU non-discrimination law) does not, by design, provide a static or homogenous framework suited to testing for discrimination in AI systems. Many of the concepts fundamental to bringing a legal claim require normative or political choices to be made by the judiciary on a case-by-case basis.
- Discrimination is, by its nature, based on human behaviour – this is manifested through negative attitudes (stereotypes, prejudice) and unintentional biases (organisational practices or internalised stereotypes). Equivalent signalling mechanisms and agency do not exist in algorithmic systems, making discrimination difficult to detect through algorithms.
- Establishing a standard set of statistical evidence for automated discrimination cases can help ensure consistent procedures for assessment, but not judicial interpretation, of cases involving AI and automated systems. The authors offer a framework for building considerations of fairness into automated systems as far as possible.

Elsewhere, interdisciplinary research based at the University of Essex (covering computer science, economics, law, philosophy, political science and sociology) has been identifying and assessing the risks and opportunities for human rights posed by AI technologies. It has proposed solutions to ensure that new technologies are designed, developed, deployed and regulated in ways that enable, rather than threaten, human rights. This has shaped landmark standards adopted by the UN Human Rights Council. The same research has also been utilised by the UK Investigatory Powers Commissioner, the Surveillance Camera Commissioner and the UK Parliament's Joint Committee on Human Rights.

Elsewhere, an evaluation of the use of socially assistive robotics (SAR) in mental health service argued that SAR should not be seen as a replacement for trained professionals nor as a panacea for all mental healthcare needs. Instead, robots can serve as clinical tools and assistants in a wide range of settings.

The creation of responsible legislation to govern AI tools will depend upon such collaborations between technological and legal expertise, informed by the broader social sciences literature.

Not only do the social sciences offer a unique perspective on governance, they are also an active ingredient in helping new technologies to be properly and fully regulated. This point is reinforced by Figure 5, which shows the number of policy documents relating to the field of law arising from grants categorised by research area. This demonstrates that the social sciences – either by themselves or through collaborative projects with STEM – have disproportionately high flows across academic boundaries, particularly because of the social science expertise on regulation.

Figure 5: Policy documents relating to the field of law arising from grants categorised by research area

Source: Dimensions from Digital Science

Most funding for research in the field of law relating to digital health technologies (including the Wachter et al., 2021 article referenced above) has been awarded by the Engineering and Physical Sciences Research Council (EPSRC). Research in the legal field arising from these grants was primarily related to the subfields of 'Law in Context' and 'Private Law and Civil Obligations' (using the ANZSRC 2020 Fields of Research), with a geometric mean FCR of 26.61 and 25.90 respectively. These publications are concerned with the justness of automated decision-making (Binns, 2020; Drake et al., 2021; Veale & Edwards, 2018), public governance of AI (Keller & Drake, 2021) and the organisational (and social) challenges of security in smart homes (Chen & Urquhart, 2021).

Such impacts, where specific social science disciplines bring to bear their expertise to inform innovation, will be critical as new technologies develop. Legal research into TAS, including artificial intelligence and consumer protection, has affected policy relating to data protection regulations (Scottish Government, 2020; Scottish Government, 2021; UK Government, 2020). But the legal field has also contributed to policy documents concerned with the ethics of algorithmic decision-making, as well as both discrimination (Grgić-Hlača et al., 2018) and digital inequality (UK Government, 2019). This intersection of expertise should be encouraged by the deliberate funding, from STEM-focused funders as well as more generalist funding agencies, of research emerging from collectives of STEM and social science researchers.

Learning points
- The social sciences are indispensable in ensuring good governance and responsible yet dynamic regulation for emerging technologies.
- Not only can social scientists and STEM work collaboratively on emerging areas of technology for the public good, they can do so in ways which are mutually beneficial and create a more effective innovation ecosystem.
- The social science component of such collaborations frequently helps new technologies to be understood and accepted by the public.

INGREDIENT 4:
Social sciences are essential to international collaboration and tackling shared global challenges

Through their insights into human relationships, societies, economies and places, and their understanding of interdependence across social, cultural, economic and political spheres, the social sciences bring a rich set of flavours. These are vital in understanding the issues, their different national contexts and the human dimensions to global challenges that are present in most of the pressing challenges. The social sciences are equally as important in helping to create, negotiate and implement global solutions to major challenges, and in monitoring the impacts of interventions on people, societies and economies.[5]

Nowhere was this more apparent in recent times than during the COVID-19 pandemic, where the social sciences and their understanding of society were critical to the efficacy of vaccine take-up, lockdown restrictions and social distancing. Later in the pandemic, insights from the social sciences also helped governments to understand COVID-19's broader impacts on mental health and wellbeing, returning to social norms in work and education settings, and longer-term shifts in behaviour, such as home working. While some of these impacts are set out in the case study below, the role of the social sciences in relation to COVID-19 has been well reported elsewhere. This report has therefore focused on different but equally important global challenges.

One of the greatest of global challenges is sustainable development, and it is often the case that both STEM and social science need to work collectively, and collaboratively, in seeking acceptable, sustainable futures, combining scientific and technical know-how with the understanding of human systems, interactions and interdependencies. As one way of illustrating this point, Figure 6 sets out the contribution of research from STEM and social science fields towards the UN's sustainable development goals (SDGs), at both a UK and global level, between 2012 and 2022.

The bar charts indicate the contribution of STEM, social science and mixed research towards SDGs relating to social, economic or environmental categories, at both a UK and global level. The measures used as a proxy for research are the number of publications (volume) and the average citation of publications (impact). Comparisons of total global and UK (authors affiliated to

---

[5] Indeed, although it has now been overtaken by political events, the UK Government's international R&I strategy would have needed to be underpinned by social sciences (such as politics, international development, geography and law). This approach would not only have assisted the nation to work effectively with international partners, it would also have provided a substantive focus for UK diplomacy and strategic advantage.

UK institutions) contributions can be seen in the top two bar graphs (Figure 6). Beneath that is the data for STEM, social science and joint STEM/social science publications and average citations, globally and for the UK.

There are some notable trends:

- A general trend that volume of publications is greater and average citation lower in the 'social' SDGs when compared with the 'economic' and 'environmental' SDGs, across all of the datasets.
- UK researchers from STEM and social sciences are active across all three SDG thematic groups.
- For UK-authored papers, about 25% of the total SDG-related publications fall into the social sciences, either uniquely or published in collaboration with STEM colleagues, and some 75% in STEM alone.
- Within each of the STEM, social science and STEM/social science subdivisions, UK-authored publications achieve significantly greater rates of citation than the global average.
- The greatest increase in citation rates (compared with the global average) for UK-authored papers – approximately double in most instances – is seen in the social science and STEM/social science publications.
- While collaboratively published studies across social science and STEM account for a minority of publications, probably for a number of different reasons, they are among the most cited research.

STEM and social science research make an important contribution to all three SDG thematic groups, and UK-published social sciences and social science/STEM research is well-cited.

Case study: Using social sciences to support COVID-19 pandemic response

Social scientific insights and social science research were essential during the COVID-19 pandemic to help policymakers and healthcare professionals take decisions which the public would support.

This was underlined at the start of the pandemic, in April 2020, in an article for the journal *Nature Human Behaviour*. Recognising that COVID-19 represented a global health crisis requiring large-scale behaviour change, the authors set out expertise on navigating threats, social and cultural influences on behaviour, science communication, moral decision-making, leadership, and stress and coping. Insights for effective response to COVID-19 for public health experts, policymakers, and community leaders included:

- The need to identify sources (for example, religious or community leaders) credible to different audiences to share public health messages – and for these to highlight bipartisan support to reduce polarisation.
- The need for more targeted public health information within marginalised communities and for public health partnerships that are internal to these communities.
- Messages that (i) emphasise benefits to the recipient, (ii) focus on protecting others, (iii) align with the recipient's moral values, (iv) appeal to social consensus or scientific norms and/or (v) highlight the prospect of social group approval tend to be persuasive.
- Preparing people for misinformation and ensuring they have accurate information and counterarguments against false information before they encounter conspiracy theories, fake news, or other forms of misinformation, can help inoculate them against false information.
- Use of the term 'social distancing' might imply that one needs to cut off meaningful interactions. A preferable term is 'physical distancing', emphasising that social connection is possible even when people are physically separated.

A paper for the Economic & Social Research Institute in Dublin examined the likelihood of people adopting behaviour changes around handwashing, face touching and social isolation in the face of a health crisis. It also emphasised the importance of clear language in reporting the pandemic in order to not sensationalise risk and undermine public trust.

Another important dimension was social sciences' ability to identify the demographics of those at most risk of COVID-19 and identify the location clusters of such groups to allow for targeted messaging and interventions. This was seen in a number of countries, including Sweden and Brazil.

Figure 6: Contribution of global and UK-based research to the United Nations Sustainable Development Goals (UN SDGs), by category of goal and category of field

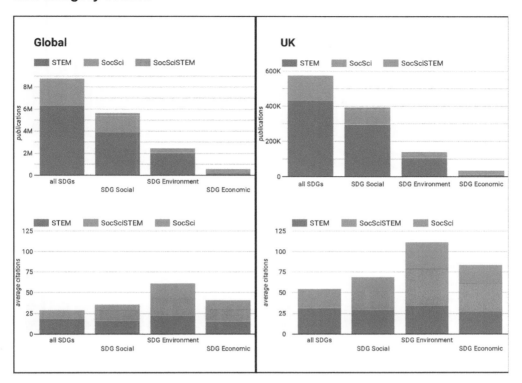

Source: Dimensions from Digital Science

Figure 7 shows the relative contribution by number of publications of the UK and global research in each field area, distributed across the UN's 17 sustainable development goals. It shows that the patterns of involvement of fields in the SDGs are generally consistent.

Figure 7: Contribution of global and UK-based research to the UN SDGs by category of research field per goal

UK SDGs

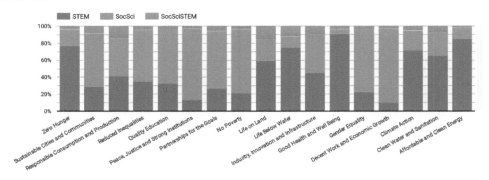

Global SDGs

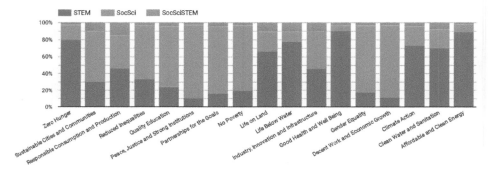

Source: Dimensions from Digital Science

Analysing the impact of research, and the respective contributions by disciplines, the UK research ecosystem is in a unique position. Based on the UK national research assessment, where the sector presents its strengths contributing to science and its impact beyond, the individual contribution by the social sciences and STEM are evident. Institutions provided evidence (in the form of underpinning research) for impact case studies which were allocated in the REF framework to eight different types of impact – defined by the area in which the impact has occurred. The bar charts in Figures 8 and 9 show the contribution of STEM and the social science fields to the REF 2021 impact case studies. In all cases, both social science and STEM fields contribute to all of the impact case study types. In five out of eight categories, the social sciences contribution, based on underpinning research, exceeds the share of STEM contributions, making the social sciences a diverse, impactful and essential base ingredient for good and socially-useful research.

Figure 8: Contribution of the STEM and social science fields to the REF Impact Case Studies by category

Share of Impact Case Studies

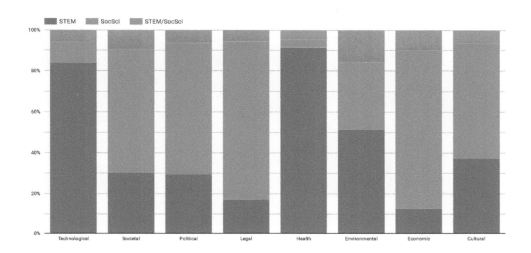

Source: Dimensions from Digital Science

Figure 9: Contribution of the STEM and social science fields to the REF Impact Case Studies by authorship and collaboration

STEM

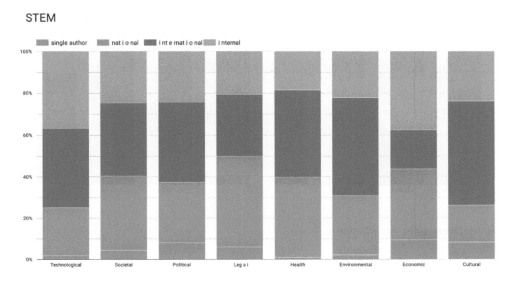

Source: Dimensions from Digital Science

Figure 9 (continued)

STEM/Social Sciences

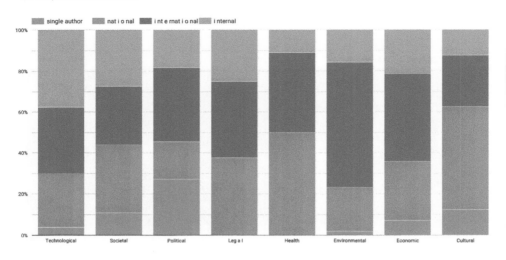

Source: Dimensions from Digital Science

Social Sciences

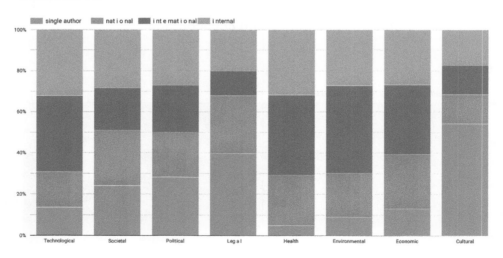

Source: Dimensions from Digital Science

Further analysis of REF 2021 impact can be found in the recent report by RAND (Stevenson et al. 2023). A further report examining the impact from SHAPE disciplines (Social Sciences, Humanities and the Arts for People and the Economy) commissioned by the Academy of Social Sciences and the British Academy will be published shortly.

Learning points
- For the UK to fulfil its global commitments and aspirations, the social sciences have a key role to play.
- UK-based research relating to the SDGs is strong across both social science and STEM in terms of citations. Further investment in research in these areas can only enhance the UK's reputation and standing as a contributor to the global research effort on the SDGs.
- While joint publications across STEM/social science are not necessarily a good indicator of the volume of multidisciplinary research that is taking place, as many researchers will prefer to publish in their discipline journals, it is clear that such publication is highly cited and worthy of strong encouragement.

Conclusions

This report has set out to explain and emphasise the vital and often under-recognised role of social science research in critical areas of our lives. We have argued that, through four 'ingredients', the social sciences are a 'secret sauce' to research from other disciplines, acting as a catalyst to create end products which are 'ready made' for wider society. Those ingredients cover four distinct areas:

1. **Social sciences enable whole-systems thinking**
2. **Social sciences are critical for good policy development**
3. **Social sciences underpin smart and responsible innovation**
4. **Social sciences are essential to international collaboration and tackling shared global challenges**

The support for these four claims is based on a range of data which point to wider trends. Case studies also provide portmanteau instances of more generalisable activity, and while these come with caveats, they add depth and texture to a broader argument based on data. The examples we have given demonstrate the essential role of the social sciences in areas that are often regarded as inhabiting the STEM sphere, such as new technologies, and the amplifying effect of collaborative work across the STEM and social science fields. Research that involves a partnership from the outset has a stronger impact on scientific citations and emerging technologies and is more useful to policymakers. Such multidisciplinarity brings the strengths of the social sciences directly to bear: questioning paradigms, anticipating unintended consequences and providing vital social, cultural and historical context.

Our most important recommendation is that such research should be better facilitated by policy that rewards projects and partnerships which cross disciplinary boundaries. This should not, of course, preclude or detract from research within specific sectors and disciplines, which is valuable in its own right. But further meeting the unfulfilled potential for cross-disciplinary research is a trend which must accelerate, as has been acknowledged by both the Grant Review and recent spending reviews. It is also an agenda which should be more visibly embraced by the devolved governments.

In order to operationalise this, we make the following recommendations which align to each of our four ingredients:

Recommendation 1: Building on the Grant Review, and recent initiatives such as <u>UKRI's cross-council responsive mode funding scheme</u>, UKRI should progressively scale up its investments in interdisciplinary research, training and leadership. These should receive further targeted support from 2025 onwards under the next Spending Review, centred on the ESRC (Economic and Social Research Council) which has a crucial role to play as a facilitator and amplifier of social science and broader transdisciplinary contributions to the wider UK R&I system.

Recommendation 2: A further round of scaled-up investment is required in policy brokerage within universities and the wider research system, building on the contribution of university policy teams, and initiatives such as then Universities Policy Engagement Network (UPEN) and Capabilities in Academic Policy Engagement (CAPE) over recent years, and the positive focusing effects of departmental Areas of Research Interest (ARIs).

Recommendation 3: Social sciences should receive greater emphasis in strategies for the responsible development, governance and regulation of new and emerging technologies – including AI. The Government Office for Science and the Department for Science, Innovation & Technology (DSIT) have a particular role to play here and need to develop more integrated strategies for engaging all disciplines in these efforts. DSIT should build on its recent Science & Technology Framework by working with partners in the social sciences to articulate a social science framework in order to reap the full benefits they offer.

Recommendation 4: The UK should ensure active participation in the remaining years of Horizon Europe and start planning now for a smooth transition into the 10th Framework Programme. The <u>recent EU–UK agreement on UK association to Horizon Europe</u> is very welcome, particularly given the framework's strong commitment to multidisciplinary social science and STEM research. The long wait for this agreement has had detrimental effects on UK research, and it will take a concerted effort on all sides to repair networks, connections and confidence levels that have suffered as a result. And preparations must start now for the next Framework Programme, which runs from 2028, to ensure that the UK is as centrally engaged as possible under its associated status. This will require sustained investment from UK funders and universities in network-building and the soft infrastructures of international collaboration. In parallel, valuable groundwork that went into the UK's Pioneer programme (as a potential alternative to association) should not be entirely lost, and elements of this broader international strategy should be salvaged and supported through further investment in the next Spending Review.

As always, the Academy of Social Sciences looks forward to engaging with policymakers and wider civil society to take forward these recommendations and to play our part.

Appendix A:
Query definitions

Keywords for Ingredient 1

Digital health technologies:
In the field of Information and Computing Sciences, title or abstract contain 'mental health' OR 'digital health technology' OR 'digital mental health'

Autonomous systems, AI and ethics:
('Autonomous System' AND 'Ethics') OR ('Autonomous System' AND 'Liability') OR ('Autonomous System' AND 'Data protection') OR ('Artificial Intelligence' AND 'Law') OR ('Artificial Intelligence' AND 'Regulation') OR ('Artificial Intelligence' AND 'Governance') OR ('Artificial Intelligence' AND 'Ethics') OR ('Artificial Intelligence' AND 'Liability') OR ('Artificial Intelligence' AND 'Data protection') OR ('Artificial Intelligence' AND 'Risk') OR ('Artificial Intelligence' AND 'Consumer Protection regulation') OR ('Artificial Intelligence' AND 'Justice') OR ('Artificial Intelligence' AND 'Accountability') OR ('AI' AND 'Governance') OR ('AI' AND 'Ethics') OR ('AI' AND 'Liability') OR ('AI' AND 'Justice') OR ('AI' AND 'Accountability') OR ('Automated Decision Making' AND 'Law') OR ('Automated Decision Making' AND 'Regulation') OR ('Automated Decision Making' AND 'Data protection') OR ('Automated Decision Making' AND 'Justice') OR ('Automated Decision Making' AND 'Accountability') OR ('Autonomous Vehicle' AND 'Law') OR ('Autonomous Vehicle' AND 'Regulation') OR ('Autonomous Vehicle' AND 'Governance') OR ('Autonomous Vehicle' AND 'Ethics') OR ('Autonomous Vehicle' AND 'Liability') OR ('Autonomous Vehicle' AND 'Data protection') OR ('Autonomous Vehicle' AND 'Risk') OR ('Autonomous Vehicle' AND 'Accountability') OR ('Autonomous Car' AND 'Regulation') OR ('Autonomous Car' AND 'Ethics') OR ('Autonomous Car' AND 'Liability') OR ('Machine learning' AND 'Governance') OR ('Machine learning' AND 'Ethics') OR ('Machine learning' AND 'Liability') OR ('Machine learning' AND 'Data governance') OR ('Machine learning' AND 'Justice') OR ('Machine learning' AND 'Accountability') OR ('Algorithm' AND 'Governance') OR ('Algorithm' AND 'Ethics') OR ('Algorithm' AND 'Data protection') OR ('Algorithm' AND 'Data governance') OR ('Algorithm' AND 'Consumer Protection regulation') OR ('Algorithm' AND 'Justice') OR ('Algorithm' AND 'Accountability') OR ('Algorithmic' AND 'Law') OR ('Algorithmic' AND 'Regulation') OR ('Algorithmic' AND 'Governance') OR ('Algorithmic' AND 'Ethics') OR ('Algorithmic' AND 'Liability') OR ('Algorithmic' AND 'Data protection') OR ('Algorithmic' AND 'Data governance') OR ('Algorithmic' AND 'Risk') OR ('Algorithmic' AND 'Consumer Protection regulation') OR ('Algorithmic' AND 'Financial Services Regulation') OR ('Algorithmic' AND 'Justice') OR ('Algorithmic' AND 'Accountability') OR ('Data' AND 'Ethics') OR ('Data' AND 'Consumer Protection regulation') OR ('Data' AND 'Financial Services Regulation') OR ('Data Protection' AND 'Law') OR ('Data Protection' AND 'Regulation') OR ('Data Protection' AND 'Governance') OR ('Data Protection' AND 'Ethics') OR ('Data Protection' AND 'Liability') OR ('Data Protection' AND 'Risk') OR ('Data Protection' AND 'Consumer Protection regulation') OR ('Data Protection' AND 'Financial Services Regulation') OR ('Data Protection' AND 'Justice') OR ('Data

Protection' AND 'Accountability')

Responsible AI:
((('Responsible AI' OR 'responsible Artificial intelligence') OR ('Explainable AI' OR 'explainable artificial intelligence') OR (Explainability) OR ('Human-Machine Teaming' AND Trust) OR ('Human-AI interaction' AND Trust) OR ('Interpretable Machine Learning' OR 'Interpretable ML') OR ('Adjustable Autonomy' OR 'Flexible Autonomy') OR ('Human-Agent Interaction' AND Trust) OR ('Trust models') OR ('Human-Robot Interaction' AND Trust) OR ('Smart Homes' AND ('Artificial Intelligence' OR AI OR Agents) AND Trust) OR ('Smart cities' AND ('Artificial Intelligence' OR AI OR 'Machine Learning' OR ML) AND Trust) OR (automated AND Trust AND Human) OR ('coalition formation' AND Trust) OR ('Agent-based Modelling' AND (Human OR Society) AND Trust) OR ('Smart Grids' AND ('Machine Learning' OR Human OR 'Artificial Intelligence' OR AI OR ML) AND Trust) OR ('Smart cities' AND ('Artificial Intelligence' OR 'Machine Learning' OR AI OR ML) AND Trust) OR (Auctions AND Trust) OR ('Game Theory' AND (Trust OR Reputation)) OR (('Human Computer Interaction' OR HCI) AND Trust))

Online learning:
('online education' OR 'online learning') OR ((educat* OR 'learning environment') AND (technolog* OR digital))

Appendix B:
Complete tables for topic-specific analysis

Table 7: Digital health technologies: UK and Global share of publications

	Publications			Average citations per publication		
	UK share of publications	UK publications	Global publications	Percentage of global average citation	UK average citations	Global average citations
Social Science Fields						
Built Environment & Design	**16.4%**	45	274	**140.3%**	18.2	13.0
Commerce, Management, Tourism & Services	**8.7%**	112	1,290	**139.3%**	20.2	14.5
Economics	**13.9%**	84	605	**105.8%**	22.8	21.6
Education	**12.6%**	254	2,018	**108.0%**	12.4	11.4
Human Society	**13.5%**	1,193	8,869	**113.7%**	16.7	14.7
Law & Legal Studies	**7.7%**	234	3,058	**127.3%**	11.3	8.9
Mixed Fields						
Environmental Sciences	**7.6%**	48	635	**174.1%**	38.3	22.0
Psychology	**14.2%**	3,633	25,619	**135.6%**	30.0	22.1

(Table 7 continued)

STEM Fields						
Agriculture, Veterinary & Food Sciences	7.8%	19	243	127.7%	25.7	20.1
Biological Sciences	12.2%	65	534	89.6%	30.2	33.7
Biomedical & Clinical Sciences	15.3%	3,128	20,484	142.7%	32.1	22.5
Chemical Sciences	8.2%	10	122	161.9%	45.1	27.9
Earth Sciences	4.1%	9	220	177.3%	20.9	11.8
Engineering	4.9%	26	526	187.8%	19.6	10.4
Health Sciences	15.4%	7,522	48,853	127.3%	22.3	17.5
Information & Computing Sciences	6.8%	426	6,259	144.6%	20.7	14.3
Mathematical Sciences	0.0%		111	176.3%	16.0	9.1
Physical Sciences	35.7%	20	56	0.0%	0.0	4.0

Table 8: Autonomous systems, AI and ethics: UK and Global share of publications

	Publications			Average citations per publication		
	UK share of publications	UK publications	Global publications	Percentage of global average citation	UK average citations	Global average citations
Social Science Fields						
Built Environment & Design	**9.7%**	86	887	**187.0%**	24.0	12.9
Commerce, Management, Tourism & Services	**7.3%**	681	9,318	**225.9%**	14.4	6.4
Economics	**10.2%**	102	1,003	**195.5%**	11.7	6.0
Education	**7.0%**	162	2,322	**216.6%**	11.2	5.2
Human Society	**11.7%**	605	5,183	**225.1%**	17.4	7.7
Law & Legal Studies	**6.3%**	680	10,786	**263.5%**	9.0	3.4
Mixed Fields						
Environmental Sciences	**7.7%**	42	547	**194.1%**	24.8	12.8
Psychology	**15.7%**	328	2,093	**173.0%**	17.4	10.0

(Table 8 continued)

STEM Fields						
Agriculture, Veterinary & Food Sciences	**14.1%**	78	552	**96.8%**	10.0	10.3
Biological Sciences	**11.5%**	209	1,823	**160.7%**	19.8	12.3
Biomedical & Clinical Sciences	**14.2%**	3,158	22,187	**157.8%**	12.3	7.8
Chemical Sciences	**8.8%**	31	353	**272.1%**	31.8	11.7
Earth Sciences	**4.4%**	34	777	**453.4%**	35.6	7.9
Engineering	**4.7%**	221	4,716	**209.4%**	18.7	8.9
Health Sciences	**19.9%**	3,174	15,961	**144.0%**	12.0	8.3
Information & Computing Sciences	**7.2%**	1,695	23,417	**188.8%**	11.5	6.1
Mathematical Sciences	**8.4%**	74	886	**165.0%**	12.0	7.3
Physical Sciences	**4.6%**	33	712	**216.5%**	14.2	6.6

Table 9: Responsible AI: UK and Global share of publications

	Publications			Average citations per publication		
	UK share of publications	UK publications	Global publications	Percentage of global average citation	UK average citations	Global average citations
Social Science Fields						
Built Environment & Design	**6.7%**	15	224	**170.4%**	14.4	8.5
Commerce, Management, Tourism & Services	**7.4%**	83	1,129	**210.3%**	18.7	8.9
Economics	**7.3%**	32	436	**244.1%**	21.2	8.7
Education	**4.1%**	4	98	**425.2%**	14.5	3.4
Human Society	**11.6%**	32	276	**277.0%**	16.2	5.8
Law & Legal Studies	**8.4%**	20	239	**145.6%**	4.6	3.2
Mixed Fields						
Environmental Sciences	**7.4%**	6	81	**263.5%**	30.8	11.7
Psychology	**11.0%**	37	337	**133.9%**	27.6	20.6

(Table 9 continued)

STEM Fields						
Agriculture, Veterinary & Food Sciences	**8.5%**	6	71	**155.2%**	11.8	7.6
Biological Sciences	**15.7%**	62	394	**155.1%**	13.4	8.6
Biomedical & Clinical Sciences	**14.8%**	149	1,006	**172.9%**	19.5	11.3
Chemical Sciences	**8.0%**	15	188	**99.2%**	6.6	6.7
Earth Sciences	**6.0%**	11	184	**161.1%**	11.0	6.8
Engineering	**7.3%**	108	1,472	**114.0%**	10.8	9.5
Health Sciences	**15.4%**	86	558	**170.5%**	26.2	15.3
Information & Computing Sciences	**6.9%**	874	12,702	**149.3%**	12.2	8.1
Mathematical Sciences	**6.1%**	14	230	**80.5%**	6.8	8.4
Physical Sciences	**6.4%**	16	250	**92.1%**	6.6	7.1

Table 10: Online Learning: UK and Global share of publications

	Publications			Average citations per publication		
	UK share of publications	UK publications	Global publications	Percentage of global average citation	UK average citations	Global average citations
Social Science Fields						
Built Environment & Design	4.4%	257	5,860	255.3%	15.8	6.2
Commerce, Management, Tourism & Services	3.7%	614	16,525	286.3%	17.4	6.1
Economics	4.5%	152	3,410	182.3%	18.3	10.0
Education	3.2%	4,094	127,455	246.9%	14.0	5.7
Human Society	4.3%	727	16,896	247.6%	14.2	5.7
Law & Legal Studies	3.2%	128	4,015	353.5%	8.0	2.3
Mixed Fields						
Environmental Sciences	5.6%	115	2,060	337.1%	28.6	8.5
Psychology	5.3%	384	7,202	184.8%	25.4	13.8

(Table 10 continued)

STEM Fields						
Agriculture, Veterinary & Food Sciences	3.5%	97	2,755	212.0%	15.4	7.3
Biological Sciences	7.6%	193	2,543	91.1%	14.4	15.8
Biomedical & Clinical Sciences	9.4%	2,234	23,725	174.1%	19.6	11.2
Chemical Sciences	5.1%	53	1,042	385.3%	33.1	8.6
Earth Sciences	2.3%	84	3,621	394.8%	16.9	4.2
Engineering	2.8%	561	19,823	255.9%	17.5	6.8
Health Sciences	8.9%	2,297	25,900	193.4%	20.1	10.4
Information & Computing Sciences	3.2%	2,253	70,886	238.8%	14.5	6.1
Mathematical Sciences	2.2%	33	1,470	199.8%	9.3	4.7
Physical Sciences	1.5%	65	4,328	325.0%	12.4	3.8

Figure 10: Concept network graph for UK research into autonomous systems, AI and ethics in the field of policy and administration (2012-2022)

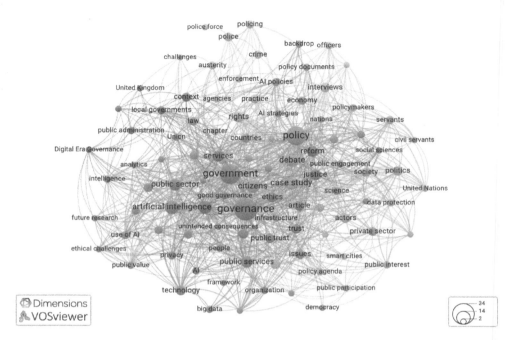

Source: Dimensions from Digital Science

Figure 10 shows that this field is concerned with both the practicalities of this technology and its governance (e.g., 'data protection', 'public administration' or 'policing'), but also the social impact (e.g., 'public value', 'citizens', 'rights', 'public trust' and 'unintended consequences'). The network also shows attention dedicated to the study of science itself: 'social science' and 'science' co-occur frequently with 'justice', 'ethics' and 'politics'.

Appendix C:
Selected bibliography of academic sources

As this report is designed primarily for the lay reader and for electronic use, we have used hyperlinks throughout the report for ease of access. In the interests of completeness, however, a fuller list of references for academic sources is included below.

Binns, R. (2020) "Human Judgment in algorithmic loops: individual justice and automated decision-making", Regulation & Governance, vol. 16, no. 1, pp 197-211.

Chen, J. & Urquhart, L. (2022) "'They're all about pushing the products and shiny things rather than fundamental security': mapping socio-technical challenges in securing the smart home", Information & Communications Technology Law, vol. 31, no. 1, pp. 99-122.

Cluver, L., Orkin, M., Gardner, F. & Boyes, E. (2012) "Persisting mental health problems among AIDS-orphaned children in South Africa", Journal of Child Psychology and Psychiatry, vol. 53, no. 4, pp. 363-370.

Cluver, L., Operario, D., Lane, T. & Kganakga, M. (2011) "'I can't go to school and leave her in so much pain': educational shortfalls among adolescent young carers in the South African AIDSepidemic", Journal of Adolescent Research, vol. 27, no. 5, pp. 581-605.

Cluver, L., Boyes, M., Orkin, M., Pantelic, M., Molwena, T. & Sherr, L. (2013) "Child-focused state cash transfers & adolescent HIV infection risks: a prospective multi-site study in South Africa", The Lancet Global Health, pp. 362-70.

Drake, A., Keller, P., Pietropaoli, I., Puri, A., Maniatis, S., Tomlinson, J., Maxwell, J., Fussey, P., Pagliari, C., Smethurst, H., Edwards, L. & Blair, W. (2022) "Legal contestation of artificial intelligence-related decision-making in the United Kingdom: reflections for policy", International Review of Law, Computers & Technology, vol. 36, no. 2, pp. 251-285.

Fankhauser, S., de Menezes, A. & Opacic, N. (2019) UK research on the social science of climate change: a synthesis of ESRC and related investments, London: Place-Based Climate Action Network / London School of Economics & Political Science.

Fonseca-Rodríguez, O., Gustafsson, P., San Sebastián, M. & Fors Connolly, A. (2021) "Spatial clustering and contextual factors associated with hospitalisation and deaths due to COVID-19 in Sweden: a geospatial nationwide ecological study", BMJ Global Health.

Grgić-Hlača, N., Redmiles, E., Gummadi, K. & Weller, A. (2018) "Human perceptions of fairness in algorithmic decision making : a case study of criminal risk prediction", in 'WWW 2018' web conference report.

Jasanoff S. (2011) "Constitutional moments in governing science and technology", Science & Engineering Ethics, vol. 17, no. 4, pp. 621-38.

Keller, P. & Drake, A. (2021) "Exclusivity and paternalism in the public governance of explainable AI", Computer Law & Security Review, vol. 40.

Lunn, P., Belton, C., Lavin, C., McGowan, F., Timmons, S. & Robertson, D. (2020) "Using behavioural science to help fight the coronavirus", ESRI Working Paper No. 656.

Mulgan, G. (2017) Anticipatory Regulation: ten ways governments can better keep up with fast-changing industries, Nesta website (accessed 20 August 2023).

Player, L., Prosser M., Thorman, D., Tirion S., Whitmarsh L., Kurz, T. & Shah, P. (2023) "Quantifying the importance of socio-demographic, travel-related, and psychological predictors of public acceptability of low emission zones", Journal of Environmental Psychology.

Poortinga, W., Demski, C. & Steentjes K. (2023) "Generational differences in climate-related beliefs, risk perceptions and emotions in the UK" Communications Earth & Environment.

Rabbitt, S., Kazdin, A., & Scassellati, B. (2015) "Integrating socially assistive robotics into mental healthcare interventions: applications and recommendations for expanded use", Clinical Psychology Review, vol. 35, pp. 35-46.

Santana Santos, V., Santos Siqueira, T., Cubas Atienzar, A. et al (2022) "Spatial clusters, social determinants of health and risk of COVID-19 mortality in Brazilian children and adolescents: a nationwide population-based ecological study", Lancet Regional Health Americas.

Stevenson, C., Grant, J., Szomszor, M., Ang, C., Kapoor, D., Gunashekar, S. & Guthrie, S. (2023) Data enhancement and analysis of the REF 2021 Impact Case Studies, California: RAND Corporation.

Stilgoe, J., Lock, S. & Wilsdon, J. (2014) "Why should we promote public engagement with science?", Public Understanding of Science, vol. 23, no. 1, pp. 4-15.

University of Essex Human Rights, Big Data and Technology Project (2021) "Operationalising Human Rights Standards in the Governance of State and Business Use of Data Analytics and Artificial Intelligence", REF 2021 Impact Case Study website (accessed 14 September 2023).

Van Bavel, J., Baicker, K., Boggio, P. et al (2020) "Using social and behavioural science to support COVID-19 pandemic response", Nature Human Behaviour, no. 4, pp. 460–471.

Veale, M. & Edwards, L. (92018) "Clarity, surprises, and further questions in the Article 29 Working Party draft guidance on automated decision-making and profiling", Computer Law & Security Review, vol. 24, no. 2, pp. 398-404.

Verfuerth, C., Gregory-Smith, D., Oates, C. J., Jones, C. R. and Alevizou, P. (2021). "Reducing meat consumption at work and at home: facilitators and barriers that influence contextual spillover", Journal of Marketing Management.

Wachter, S., Mittelstadt, B. & Russell, C. (2021) "Why Fairness Cannot Be Automated: bridging the gap between EU non-discrimination law and AI", Computer Law & Security Review, no. 41.

Whitmarsh, L. (2022) "Tackling climate change requires profound societal transformation", Campaign for Social Science website (accessed 20 August 2023).

Williams, R. (2006) "Compressed foresight and narrative bias: pitfalls in assessing high technology futures", Science as Culture, vol. 15, no. 4, pp. 327-348